Emotional Strength Explained

A NEW way of responding to emotional life: A Workbook

Alicia Pozsony

ISBN – 978-0-578-98245-8

Copyright 2021

All Rights Reserved. No part of this publication may be reproduced, stored in a retrieval system, distributed, or transmitted by any means (electronic, mechanical, photocopying, or recording, or otherwise) in any form without prior explicit written permission of the author.

This is a self-help workbook.

This is also a work of creative nonfiction. The views expressed in this memoir are solely those of the author.

This book contains stories relating to sensitive issues and the author has taken lengthy steps to ensure the material is presented in a compassionate and respectful manner.

DEDICATION

This book is dedicated to

My mother, Robin (Pearce) Baron whom without I'd not be as strong. It was her love and perseverance despite hard challenges, that taught me to always hope, never give up and "Do my best".

My mentor, Joanie Sanches who taught me above all that we all need to live our truth and follow our own soul journey to achieve balance and harmony.

Steven Cuoco, the most positive and real person I know, who builds others up and makes everyone he encounters full of hope and greatness!

Michael Pozsony, without his love, wisdom and insight, I'd not be who I am today.

Author's Note

People have asked me how I do it. They say, "How do you stay so strong and still so kind?" and "After you have been through all you have, how do you stay on track?"

They have said, "I would not have been able to make so many good choices if I were in your shoes."

This got me thinking about how I got here.

Developing **Emotional Strength** played a major role.

You do not have to just "go through it"…

you can **Grow** through it.

I hope this workbook will serve you well again and again and inspire you to become healthier and more **Emotionally Strong**.

Emotional Strength Workbook

THIS BOOK Belongs to:

_____

A brave, courageous, and strong person willing to make changes and be open to the possibilities that await!

Emotional Strength Workbook

CONTENTS

About **Emotional Strength** 1

Before you Begin 4

Build **Emotional Strength** 9

Face it! 13

Reject Criticism and Judgement 21

Redefine Health 24

Feel the Real 28

Find Solutions 34

Define Healthy People to Support You 39

Feel your Emotions More Deeply 41

Move Forward 46

Be Brave Enough to Face Yourself- DECIDE 48

Functional Improvement 51

Squash the Doubt and Allow Yourself to be Self-Confident 54

Be Open & Live an Inspired Life 56

Keep it up! 58

Find Inspiration & Stories of Hope 61

    Paraplegic Veteran makes a difference 63

    I Tapped into My Support System 64

    My Reflection 65

    10 Secrets for Success & Inner Peace 67

    The Power of Thoughts and Imaginations 70

    The Power of 10 72

Support Mind, Body & Spirit 73

Tracking Your Progress 79

About **Emotional Strength**

Welcome to the Human Condition.

Life can get you down. And once you are down, you may have heard people tell you to "keep your chin up" or "be strong" but what they really mean is that you should use your **Emotional Strength** to help yourself. This may very well be the thing you see in others that you are missing. You may be in a situation and come out of it feeling down or depressed. You might be thinking, there is a better way.

For some, **Emotional Strength** may seem like having control over your emotions. For others, it is being able to understand and feel your emotions.

Let's look at the definition of **Emotional Strength**:

> "The ability to respond in an open and vulnerable way in the face of intense emotional experience, feeling one's way deeper into the emotion which allows access to implicit functional processes driving action."

Explained simply:

> **"Emotional Strength is the response you have when reacting to events.** Emotional strength also helps you to navigate difficult circumstances and influences so many areas of your behavior."

Emotional strength is something we all must practice and strengthen so life doesn't creep up and wreck havoc.

Different from psychology practices of turning a negative experience into a positive one, the core of practicing emotional intelligence is to honestly and deeply feel the emotional experience - And allow yourself to be vulnerable. This helps you open your emotional responses and change the way you understand your emotions in daily life. Just like the first time you rode a bike or tried something new. You might not have succeeded the first time, but as you did it more and more, you got better and gained confidence. When you did fall after hitting a curb or riding over loose gravel, you were able to get back on the bike again without too much trouble. Emotional strength must be practiced and maintained.

As defined by Sciencedirect.com:

- **Emotional Strength** is proposed as a new way of responding to emotional life.

- **Emotional Strength** involves an open and vulnerable response to intense emotional experience.

- **Emotional Strength** involves feeling one's way deeper and further into emotion.

- **Emotional Strength** allows access to implicit functional processes driving action.

Before you Begin

You may have heard about some of the things in this book before. The difference with this approach is that it is a targeted approach that when done in order completely, brings real change because it is concentrated and focused. Instead of operating from a naive, unsure state or a people pleasing state where you look for immediate gratification, practicing things to bring you **Emotional Strength** allows you to be **stronger**, more confident, and less needy.

There are lines in this workbook for writing and white space for notes or doodling. Use this workbook as you.'d like- it is meant to be as unique as you.

> *"Did you know that every single time you have a thought your brain releases biochemicals that flood throughout your body? You can feel cold and shaky when you experience sadness or anxiety, or you can feel hot and flushed when you become angry. We are so fortunate that our bodies are consistently trying to communicate with us when we are sad angry or happy and it all starts in your <u>brain</u>. Your brain is also the organ of happiness. So that you can increase the level of happiness in your life, it is crucial for you to know how to talk back to your Automatic Negative Thoughts (ANTs) that pop up. By challenging these negative thoughts, you take away their power and take control of your moods."*
>
> by Daniel G Amen, MD

Things to keep in mind as you use this workbook

We all like to write about what we want, what makes us feel good, and what matters most to us. When you do this, you are manifesting and putting the positivity out there.

- Setting goals helps you to write it down and hold yourself accountable.
- How you may have survived overwhelming circumstances, by just putting one foot in front of the other, is not something that can be handled properly all at once. Taking a step-by-step approach will help you stay present and do your best.
- Most of the strength-building will come from your trials. Be proactive about for the best outcome.
- Keep the dialogue going with yourself. This is good because becoming vulnerable begins with self-talk and self-love. This is all self-awareness-building work that will bring you **Emotional Strength**.
- Befriending yourself is an excellent way to befriend others. Setting boundaries begins with us and extends outward to create balance and a strong center.
- Caring enough to be honest about the hard stuff will grow your **Emotional Strength**.

- Reading about stories of hope build inspiration and connection to the world.
- You can begin and begin again at any time. This is a journey, not a once and done.

REMEMBER:

You are elegant, attractive, and talented; therefore, you have great potential for helping others, *including yourself.*

You are a creative, independent, and capable person that knows the importance of planning.

You can be enterprising and create a safe and certain outcome.

You are strong, impressive and can be friendly.

You can stand out and be visible while still being true to yourself.

Emotional Strength Workbook

Build Emotional Strength

"Put yourself first.

It's the most important tool when it comes to self-care."

-Steven Cuoco

Certified Emotional Intelligence Specialist

To build **Emotional Strength**, you must be honest and ask yourself:

"What needs improving?"

Now that you know what **Emotional Strength** is, be open and ask yourself:

"How can I build my own **Emotional Strength**?"

Believe it or not, regardless of your age or your situation, there are just **a few things you need to know that you can use in your daily life** to help you develop and maintain **Emotional Strength**.

This workbook is designed to walk you through exactly where you are today and bring you to a place of **Emotional Strength** and certainty.

It is meant for you to take your time and read each line thoroughly.

Then, let it sit with you. Let is resonate with you to the unconscious parts of yourself that you so easily normally let slip by.

Through the cycle of self-analysis, you will gain self-awareness. Then you can determine how you can become stronger emotionally.

This self-awareness also makes you more intelligent and able to better navigate your own life, feeling more alive and truer to yourself and to those you care about.

Emotional Strength Workbook

1. **First, think about what made you pick up this book. It might have been because you have felt as humans sometimes do, imperfect and in need of something to improve your situation.**

   List the FIRST thing that needs improving in your life:

   _____
   _____
   _____
   _____

   List ANOTHER thing that needs improving in your life:

   _____
   _____
   _____
   _____

   List ANY OTHER things that need improving in your life:

   _____
   _____
   _____
   _____
   _____
   _____
   _____

Stop. Think about where you are in the situation. Believe you can improve it. Come back tomorrow and continue to the next step.

Face it!

Next, the simple but tough part. When you are in the middle of something, it's not easy to rise above it. It's not easy to see yourself from another perspective.

First, become strong. What this really means is you need to open your mind to see yourself as you really are. No, not the face you see when you look in the mirror, or the person you think you are or the person you want to be. Not just the person with all the feelings and thoughts, but **that person everyone else sees**.

Be open to seeing who you really are, shortcomings and all. Acquaintances and people that are not in your inner circle may not tell you what they really think of you. Therefore, you are left to your own perceptions of what they think. We may sugar coat it, and tell ourselves, we are fine. We do this because it protects us and makes us feel better. It's easier. By not relying on the emotional strength allows you to not face the things about ourselves, those things we might not want to deal with, but need to.

At this point, ask how the changes you want to make in yourself will impact others, and how they may perceive you.

Once you have the strength and bravery to be open to see things you may not want to see, you are ready for the next thing.

Ready? (Answer honestly! If you are not ready, come back tomorrow.)

Me as others might see me:

_____
_____
_____
_____
_____
_____
_____
_____
_____
_____
_____
_____
_____
_____
_____
_____
_____
_____
_____
_____
_____
_____
_____

Emotional Strength Workbook

_____
_____
_____
_____
_____
_____
_____
_____
_____

Remember there are many types of people running their own games, so it is important to have a **strong core**. Taking steps to present a more emotionally strong persona is not easy because emotional insecurities run deep in our core and are not easily healed. Our core can be strengthened through the work you will put in through this book. List games people around you play or manipulations they may try. What is your reaction? If you back away or ignore it or make excuses for them, think about what will change if you change. (You may need to pull in some spiritual strength for this step.)

List them here.

_____
_____
_____
_____
_____
_____

Emotional Strength Workbook

Next, think of the healthiest person you know.

What does that look like? Are they exercising? Eating right? Are they popular? Do they have more style than you? More money than you?

List of what healthy people look like:

_____
_____
_____
_____
_____
_____
_____
_____
_____
_____
_____
_____
_____
_____
_____
_____

Are you that far off from what is important to you?

Now, you must know that we are all born into some things that we cannot change. Other things are learned or are organic.

This may be a tough fact to accept. This may be something that might make you bitter or resentful. That star QB or head cheerleader back in school had what you and I didn't have. Maybe it's some you know even today. Maybe it is the looks, or the personality they have. Maybe it was some other reason, something you just didn't understand.

It's important to accept this so you can move beyond it and see what you yourself have to offer. When answering this, you may want to go back to the mirror again to see what else may come up.

List of things that are difficult for me to accept:

_____
_____
_____
_____
_____
_____
_____
_____
_____
_____
_____

Emotional Strength Workbook

_____
_____
_____

Life happens in stages.

~

Understand you are embarking on a change of growth. Please keep in mind, however, that if, in the past, if you have done things to change yourself or a situation, and it did not turn out how you had hoped, keep in mind that there are some situations when things may not seem right no matter what you do.

When nothing is falling into place, you must know that some people are just not "your people". Secondarily, know your strength comes from within. Pull from that, and keep moving forward, even if it is just one step at a time. It may be difficult to accept this. Spend some time on acceptance.

Come back tomorrow and think more about some things you can do different to move forward.

List how you will move forward, for you, intentionally and with confidence today:

_____
_____

Emotional Strength Workbook

Reject Criticism and Judgement

Take this time to consider whether you accepted other people's judgement or if you have held grudges.

Accepting criticism and judgment and holding grudges will not improve your **Emotional Strength**. Also, consider a situation that is passively or openly abusive. Some call this "toxic".

List of judgements or criticisms I let affect me:

_____
_____
_____
_____
_____
_____
_____
_____
_____
_____
_____
_____
_____
_____

_____
_____
_____
_____
_____
_____
_____
_____
_____
_____
_____
_____
_____
_____
_____

After a day or so, please revisit and promise yourself how you will react differently to criticism and judgement.

Leave situations that are abusive and make you want to run or hide.

_____
_____
_____
_____
_____
_____
_____

Emotional Strength Workbook

Redefine Health

Now, look at what might be healthy for you.

Maybe it is cutting down on sugar or switching to diet soda or vaping or smoking less. Decide to change just one thing every week.

Facing this desire to change will help you on your journey to **Emotional Strength** because it will show that you are capable of growth.

If you commit to get stronger emotionally, it means you will try and fail and get stronger in the process.

Something as simple as giving up chocolate for a week works until you get stressed and reach for it again or eat a dessert because you are out to dinner makes you try again the next Monday. You will see strength with yourself grow by doing this over and over with different things at varying scale. The main thing is not to give up!

List of changes I can make (no matter how small):

_____

_____

Emotional Strength Workbook

_____
_____
_____
_____
_____
_____
_____
_____

If you are not sure where to start, start by listing daily ways you can be Grateful.

> "Gratitude makes sense of our past, brings peace for today, and creates a vision for tomorrow."

_____
_____
_____
_____
_____
_____
_____
_____
_____

_____

_____

_____

_____

_____

Stop.

After a day, set timelines to these so that each week, make just one change at a time. Elicit help from a trusted friend, mentor, life coach, or therapist as needed. This will help you make it real. You will build honesty with yourself and build your emotional toughness.

_____

_____

_____

_____

_____

Timing is crucial.

If you rush it or rush into it, you are more likely to go back to your bad habits, whereas if you take time, you can grow into consistently making the right choices.

List of changes I will start to make (you can list your start and stop dates and successes and failures and important things you learn here, too):

_____

_____

_____

_____

_____

_____

_____

_____

_____

_____

_____

_____

_____

_____

_____

_____

Feel the Real

Accept it! Don't make excuses.

What didn't you get?

Think about the situations and changes you are making. Were you treated unfairly? Are you feeling sorry for yourself? Are you stuck thinking about something (or someone) that makes you have self-doubt? Developing **Emotional Strength** requires you to have healthy thoughts and actions. **List the things you didn't get from others or from a situation that makes you hold on to those negative feelings:**

_____
_____
_____
_____
_____
_____
_____
_____
_____
_____
_____

_____

_____

_____

_____

_____

_____

_____

_____

_____

_____

_____

_____

_____

_____

_____

OK, so what?! Allow yourself to be accepting and know you can move on.

Forgive when needed.

Let go, Let God and move on.

Stop.

> WHEN YOU *need*,
> GOD *knows*.
> WHEN YOU *ask*,
> GOD *listens*.
> WHEN YOU *believe*,
> GOD *works*.

THOUGHTS:

_____
_____
_____
_____
_____
_____
_____
_____
_____
_____
_____
_____
_____
_____

More Thoughts:

After you wake up the next day, choose your spiritual power and do one daily practice each day and it will reinforce your faith, and your comfort in it, despite what you went through.

Note your daily practices that help with the different things you are becoming accepting of. Note any forgiveness you see happening:

_____
_____
_____
_____
_____
_____
_____
_____
_____
_____
_____
_____
_____
_____
_____
_____
_____
_____
_____
_____
_____

Emotional Strength Workbook

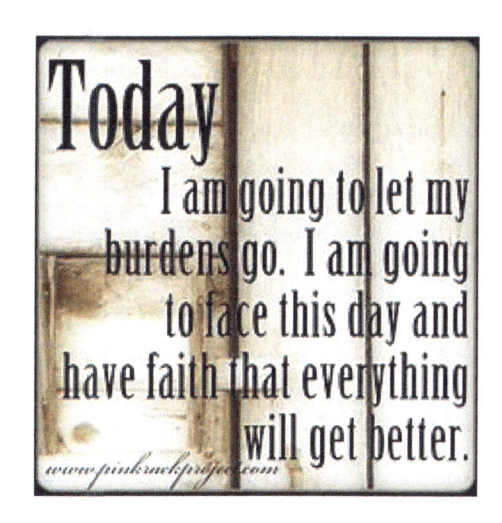

_____
_____
_____
_____
_____
_____
_____
_____
_____
_____

> Today I am going to let my burdens go. I am going to face this day and have faith that everything will get better.
>
> *www.pinkrackproject.com*

Find Solutions

Now you know what you didn't get.

Don't let your experiences define you, let them **improve** you.

Begin A G A I N!

Here are some examples:

1. You couldn't keep a job – means you haven't found the right fit. It IS out there. Stay positive, and keep looking.

2. You came from a broken home- means you know what it's like to be different and that has made you strong. Or worse, it has made you bitter or angry. You may be hurting but it doesn't have to mean you cannot start now.

List of experiences that affected you emotionally negatively and what you wanted from them:

_____
_____
_____
_____
_____
_____
_____
_____

_____

_____

_____

_____

_____

_____

_____

_____

_____

_____

_____

_____

By now, you are practicing positivity, growing, and changing and able to put your **Emotional Strength** to work.

Stop.

After a day, try to brainstorm solutions to the outcomes where you were left drained or struggling.

Understand there may not be solutions to all situations.

List of ways you could have come differently out of those situations that negatively affected you:

_____
_____
_____
_____
_____
_____
_____
_____
_____
_____
_____
_____
_____
_____
_____
_____

Emotional Strength Workbook

_____
_____
_____
_____
_____
_____
_____
_____

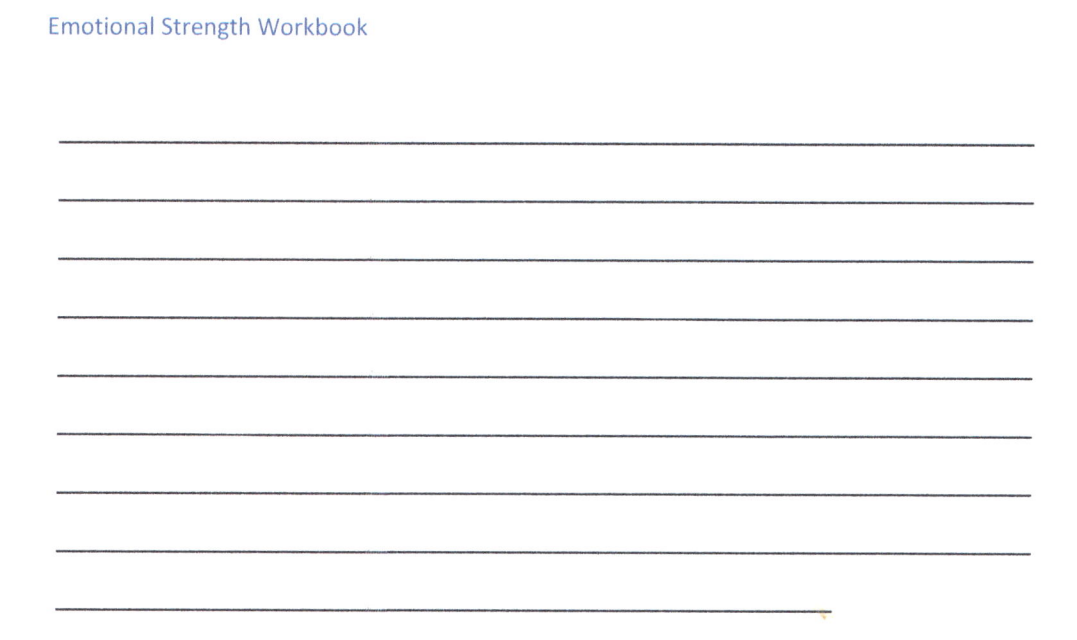

Nice work! These are the tools you are building in your emotional toolkit!

Repeat after me: **"I stand grounded and do not have to let emotions control my actions."**

Pause, Reflect, and Move Forward

Define Healthy People to Support You

"Surround yourself with people who want the best for you because they want the best for themselves."

-STEVEN CUOCO
CERTIFIED EMOTIONAL INTELLIGENCE SPECIALIST

You need a support system. So, recognize that. Start by making a list of people in your life that are healthy. List people from your past, like a teacher you had or some other person from your past – remember the thing they taught you.

If you have no healthy people, then it's time to re-prioritize healthy. Make that an action plan. Support can come in the form of something healthy like a mantra, or from a meme or that you read online, social media or seen on television.

List of healthy people and topics that can help you remain emotionally strong:

_____
_____
_____
_____
_____
_____

Feel your Emotions More Deeply

~

Fear runs deep where instability has made its mark. It creates an inability to trust oneself.

Maybe you don't know what you didn't get so you don't know how it has affected you.

Maybe you had a condescending parent and didn't realize how it beat down on your conscience and your confidence.

Maybe you had an absentee parent, and if not for their own choice or something else outside their control, may have played out very different in your world.

Maybe you are in an unhappy marriage – Believe you can get back to where you once were.

~

Ask for help. Trust someone and let down the walls. This will help you understand what makes you not want to change.

There are many things that can easily improve your problems.

Compromise is always at the heart of it.

Agree to **listen the right way**.

List your feeling on this below.

Maybe you have **a job** that is **going nowhere**.

Have you decided is it just not a good fit?

It's OK to not be good at something. Don't stay. Free yourself and your mind to be open to the right fit for you.

Is it a boss, manager or co-worker who is the problem?

You are not going to get along with everyone. You're not. If you are lucky, you found out at a young age that there was someone who didn't like you and hopefully you had the support to be able to learn from that and realize you are lucky and can find your people… your "tribe" as they say. It is true – there is a big world out there. Don't give up. Learn from each day and each new situation.

Is the work too hard? What is it about the work that is not a match? Have a conversation with your boss. Speaking openly and candidly can help you, as well as help them, to understand the situation and get clarity about yourself.

List your deeper feelings below about what you didn't get:

_____
_____
_____
_____
_____
_____

_____
_____
_____
_____
_____
_____
_____
_____
_____
_____
_____
_____
_____
_____
_____
_____
_____
_____
_____

Stop.

After a day, go back and list why you should hold your head up high.

List the thing that you will replace that with (like a skill, hobby, or accomplishment, for some examples). Trust Yourself instead of the thoughts or feelings of others as you may have done in the past.

Emotional Strength Workbook

- **Consider using a Gratitude Journal – Writing things that you are grateful will help you forgive others over time.**

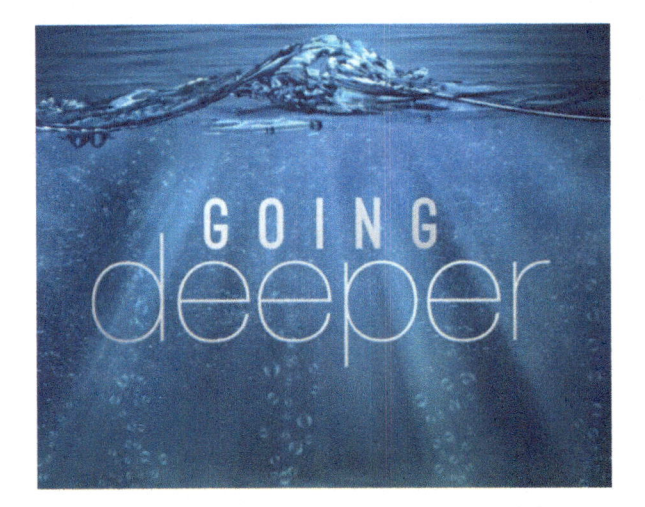

Move Forward

Ask what you think you can do now to move forward and continue nurturing yourself in new healthier ways. **Answer here:**

_____
_____
_____
_____
_____
_____
_____
_____
_____
_____
_____
_____
_____
_____
_____
_____
_____
_____
_____
_____

_____
_____
_____
_____
_____
_____

Emotional Strength Workbook

Be Brave Enough to Face Yourself- DECIDE

You identified who you are in step 1, and you came up with some solutions. Now, it's time to face yourself and decide.

It's your life, decide how you want to live it.

Go through a process to face yourself. **Ask yourself who and how you want to be today.**
List it here:

_____
_____
_____
_____

Use this skill each day.

Keep writing, watch webinars, listen to podcasts, and read about what makes sense for you to be your best self. Revisit the section above when you feel you are changing or getting stronger to continually test your improved **Emotional Strength**.

Functional Improvement

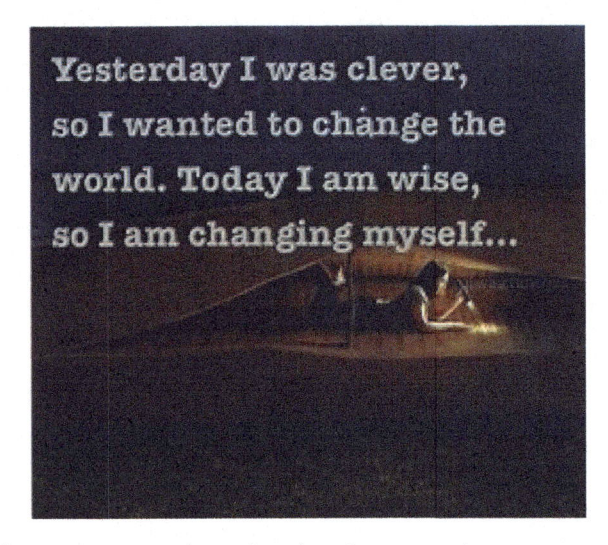

> Yesterday I was clever, so I wanted to change the world. Today I am wise, so I am changing myself...

Ask yourself what you must do to be that improved person.

"Getting in touch with ourselves is a gift we give ourselves."

-JOANIE SANCHES

AUTHOR

Let this book and especially this section be an ever-evolving tool – put in time and effort for just what you are ready to work on.

Most people will shrug this off quicker than they even realize; dare I say it, GIVE UP!! "No, I'm not going to take time to try harder and talk to and be more kind to more people." "I'm not quitting smoking / vaping. That's too much work, and plus, my friend is doing it and they will look at me differently." If your views are similar, you are not there yet. You are not ready and that is okay. Maybe you just need more time to get stronger. Go back to Chapter 1.

If you are thinking "I don't want to find better company. The friends are who I have, and they already know me." If your views are similar, you are not there yet. You are not ready and that is okay. Maybe you just need more time to get stronger. Go back to Chapter 1.

If you tell yourself "This is going to take coming out of my comfort zone." If your views are similar, you are not there yet. You are not ready and that is okay. Maybe you just need more time to get stronger. Go back to Chapter 1.

Unlock Yourself. Free Your Spirit. Change Your Life.

Things I can change to be more like the person I want to be:

_____
_____
_____
_____

Squash the Doubt and Allow Yourself to be Self-Confident

To reach your goal, you must let go of any self-doubt. Let go of the habit of telling yourself comforting reassuring thoughts. Instead, imagine the possibilities of how much better you can become.

Self confidence & Doubt

- Am I able to do it?
- Am I good enough?
- Will I be successful?
- Will I make it?
- Can I do it?
- Am I ready?

Technique — YES! / NO!
Strategy — YES! / NO!
Mental toughness — YES! / NO!
Physical preparation — YES! / NO!

If you can be open and work at the things you listed above and within this workbook, you will start to have the trait of someone with **Emotional Strength** – have comfort in who you are and what you enjoy.

Repeat this section as many times and for as many things no matter how small.

Be Open & Live an Inspired Life

Now that you have proven you can feel your emotions and be functionally stronger, you are asking how might you live a more inspired life?

To become enlightened, you need to ask the questions:

1. What matters most?
2. What fulfills you?
3. What gives your life meaning?
4. What do you really want?

Your answers might surprise you, but you need to be open to accept it. Write them below.

_____
_____
_____
_____
_____
_____
_____
_____
_____
_____
_____

Draw something representative of yourself:

Keep it up!

"Find out what a person needs, not what they want. When you find out what someone needs, you can do it or offer it at the highest level and with trust. That's when you become an asset and someone they don't want to replace or live without."

-STEVEN CUOCO,

CERTIFIED EMOTIONAL INTELLIGENCE SPECIALIST

To become happier and more carefree, you need to not be afraid to begin to take care of yourself:

Trust the unknown.

Put your own mental health first.

Put your physical health first.

Put your spiritual health first.

Let go and be open to learn something.

Doing all these things repeatedly for different situations you encounter, will ensure you are continually getting stronger emotionally.

Pay attention to how you are growing. List them here:

_____
_____
_____
_____

Emotional Strength Workbook

25 things you can CONTROL

#1 How you respond to challenges.

#2 Who you ask for help.

#3 WHEN YOU ASK FOR HELP.

#4 Saying you Need a break.

#5 HOW YOU act.

#6 How much effort you put to something.

#7 Getting enough sleep.

#8 Completing your responsibilities.

#9 Using an i-Statement.

#10 saying what you need.

#11 How much exercise you do.

#12 Setting your boundaries.

#13 Respecting the personal space of others.

#14 When and if you forgive others.

#15 HOW OFTEN YOU SMILE.

#16 owning up to your mistakes.

#17 Whether or not you accept yourself.

#18 Whether you look for the negatives or positives.

#19 What you focus on in this very moment.

#20 What goals you create for yourself.

#21 THE KIND OF ATTITUDE YOU HAVE.

#22 How you relate to you feelings.

#23 Whether you help someone out or not.

#24 How you take care of and treat your body.

#25 WHEN YOU SHOW EMPATHY.

Find Inspiration & Stories of Hope

In Chapter 1 I talked about what is healthy to you. There are many stories that will help you find hope through the lives of others. Each person is different but one thing that is the same: We can all be humble and persevere if we try.

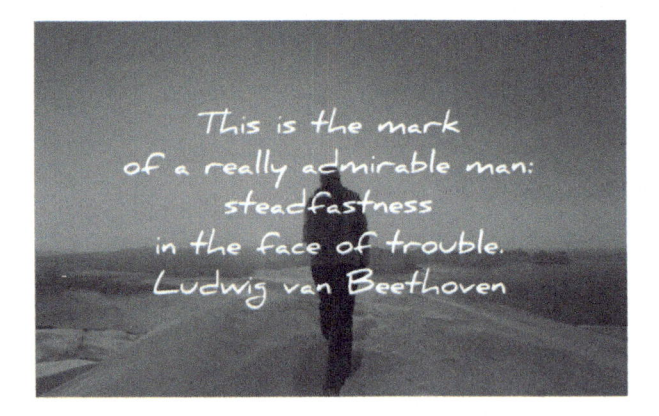

> This is the mark of a really admirable man: steadfastness in the face of trouble.
> Ludwig van Beethoven

Add your story here:

_____

_____

_____

_____

Emotional Strength Workbook

Paraplegic Veteran makes a difference

For me, unhealthy was when I was in my early twenties, and I started sleeping for more hours than I'd like to remember. I didn't realize what was happening for a long time. Friends started asking questions. I began writing things down. I was beside myself. I used logic to talk through what was happening. I thought I could fix it. When that didn't help, I was trying to see what was affecting me outside myself that was causing it. I looked at other people and tried to see how I was different from them. Maybe it was my eating habits. So I tried to be normal. I tried to go to sleep that same time every night. I tried to eat better. I tried exercise. I noticed my moods were up and down and no matter what, I still slept 12 hours a day. My friends kept trying to get me out, but I kept saying no more and more. I couldn't help it and I didn't care. My job was affected.

I needed to face myself and accept something outside of myself.

For agonizing month after month for up to 2 years, it took something my uncle said – "Just ACT!!!" My uncle was disabled in a Veteran hospital 1800 miles away and was emailing me through a kind stranger who volunteered to help. You see, he could no longer use his hands or fingers to type, nor his legs to walk. This simple command made me want to be open enough to change.

I finally realized through my closest friend that I needed medication to treat my odd and inappropriate behavior. This this was depression. This was not me.

After a year of taking Prozac and working a good job, I was able to beat it by establish healthy roles, giving up unhealthy relationships, foods and drinks and moving beyond what held me back.

*It's important to listen to your trusted advisors especially if they are telling you something that may help you. Changes may be difficult at first, but remember, better to try something different to see the outcome than not trying at ll.

I Tapped into My Support System

I woke that day feeling stressed out and especially alone. I felt hopeless because no matter what I did to feel better, nothing better happened. Just then, I got a text.

"Happy Friday"

It was my friend. She convinced me to get up, face the day and meet her for lunch. I did, but my heart was not in it.

In the first ten minutes, I learned she had been struggling too! The stress of dealing with her family non-stop since the COVID Pandemic during quarantine had her struggling big-time. We agreed, that day, to promise to walk daily and be there to help each other through.

*Supportive relationships are powerful because they activate immune functioning, boost mood, and reduce pain. Expand your support system by reaching out – Don't isolate, even when that feels like the best thing to do.

My Reflection

I was feeling fine. Everything seemed normal. In fact, it was a good day. I said good morning and goodbye to my household. I texted a friend, I went to work. I said hello to a colleague. Then, I joined a meeting, with the camera on. I saw my image, compared to others. We were all different. I felt good being a 40-something female. I knew I was doing my best to care for myself - I exercised, I ate right (well, mostly) and I tried to care for myself and others. Then, on that day like any other, it hit me: On the inside who I was, was not who I was on the outside. On that camera that day, I saw that little girl, who was abandoned as a child and neglected and not given all she deserved. Despite all she did to survive and strive, as a fully grown adult, she could not truly become someone different without dealing with her issue. It was time to deal. She was ready.

10 Secrets for Success & Inner Peace

by Wayne Dyer

~

Secret #1 Have a mind that is open to everything attached to nothing.

When you are truly open minded, you open yourself up to the potential and possibility that everything and anything is available to you. Often the very things we need to do to have what we want is in that which we reject because our minds are closed to alternatives and different points of view.

A mind that is truly open to everything will also help you to move beyond a lot of the conflicts you experience in your life. An open mind can listen to and even accept other people and their beliefs without judgement.

Secret #2 Don't die with your music still in you.

The music that you hear inside of you urging you to take risks and follow your dreams is your intuitive connection to the person in your heart.

Secret #3 You can't give away what you don't have.

By changing your inner thoughts to the higher frequencies above from kindness peace joy, you'll attract more of the same and you'll have those higher energies to give away.

Secret #4 Embrace silence.

Silence reduces fatigue and allows you to experience your own creative juices.

Secret #5 Give up your personal history.

Secret #6 You can't solve a problem the same mind that created it.

Results are source for everything in your life.

Secret #7 There are no justified resentments.

Anytime you are turning the controls over to others to manipulate, you take away from yourself. Angry people live in an angry world, sad people live in a sad world and happy people live in a happy world.

No matter how much someone has wronged you, you simply cannot justify the resentment because ultimately it will only hurt you and drain your energy on something incredibly debilitating.

Secret #8 Treat yourself as if you already are what you'd like to be.

From thoughts to feelings to actions, they will react affirmatively when you stay inspired and get out in front of yourself in ways that are consistent with what you want to become. Whether you think it is impossible or not, either way, you'll be on the right track.

Secret #9 Treasure your Divinity

You are a piece of the divine intelligence – that supports everything. There is an aspect to every one of us that is invisible, yet very real. You are a divine creation of God and therefore you can never be separated from that which created you.

God exists within you and you don't need to go and look anywhere but inside to find God. This divine part of your life is not only a 'part' of you but makes up the very essence of who you are as a human being.

Learning to treasure it will help you to value yourself and life for the magnificence that it really is.

Secret #10 Wisdom is avoiding all thoughts that weaken you.

Every thought you have will either strengthen or weaken you. Thoughts of force will always weaken you because it requires a counter force.

Thoughts of peace, joy, love and acceptance will empower you for they don't create a counter force and it stems from a willingness to allow the world to be as it is.

Wisdom is about learning this great truth and really living it in every aspect of your life.

Emotional Strength Workbook

The Power of Thoughts and Imaginations

by Dr. Bwawna Gautam

If we cannot stop someone's hurtful actions, can we change the way we feel about it?

We come across many different people in life and we don't get along with each and every person. There are people who are our biggest critics and find fault in everything we do. There are situations when we have a choice to remove those people from our lives, but sometimes these people are part of our surroundings - it can be your family member, a relative, a colleague or anyone else that you cannot avoid. Some people will always try to belittle you, challenging your self-worth. It can be very painful when those harsh words come from those who are around you or the ones you trust. You cannot change their actions, but you can always change the way you <u>react</u> to their criticism so that they no longer get the pleasure of provoking you. Trust yourself and remember - no one knows you more than you know yourself. Never anyone control your life. Only you should control how you feel about yourself.

Strength

It is the courage we find during life's most difficult times that makes our souls grow

Adele Basheer

The Power of 10

If you start to feel overwhelmed, anxious or hurt or ashamed, gain a new perspective: Ask whether this will really matter in 10 minutes, 10 days, 10 weeks, 10 months or 10 years. This can help you prioritize what matters most and let go of the rest.

Support Mind, Body & Spirit

You have done a lot of work so far. Be proud!

Now, how to stay where you are and not fall backward?

First, understand it's healthy to say no. Saying no is simply setting a boundary. If it makes someone uncomfortable or mad, there are ways to handle it that will not ruin the relationship.

First, make sure they know it is a boundary. Give them time after you state your boundary.

They may be angry and act like you are wrong. Stand strong. Remember you are being true to yourself. This is a healthy lifestyle change.

After a day, or few days, approach them again. This should be enough time to get to the root of the issue and go one or two levels deeper in understanding how to be in a place where you both can be content.

Notice I didn't say happy?

You may feel happy and yet they may still be unhappy. This shift may take some care and feeding so remember to keep communication open.

List of boundaries you need to make (and steps to keep the relationship intact, if appropriate):

_____
_____
_____
_____
_____
_____
_____
_____
_____
_____
_____
_____
_____
_____
_____
_____
_____
_____
_____
_____
_____
_____

_____

_____

Communicate with them to check the pulse – meaning talk about things along the way to show you care.

Next, open yourself up to others to learn what real friendship, love, trust, sincerity, and genuineness feels like. When you open your heart, you live from a place of richness and clarity versus skepticism and insecurity. The clarity will give you the wisdom to judge the situations you encounter from a place of **Emotional Strength** instead of a place of low vibration.

Communicate with yourself to ensure you remind yourself of this very important and good self-care that you are actively performing. It may feel odd but as time passes, you may feel an inner strength that will leave you feeling supported and stronger.

Ways to keep communication open and people in my life and myself:

_____
_____
_____
_____
_____
_____
_____
_____

Emotional Strength Workbook

Now, remind yourself your body is your temple. BE kind to it. Within your physical body lies your soul and whether you realize it or not, you are continuing your lifelong journey. You will need to make choices that may not be easy but are for the good of your body, so it aligns with your spirit. Consider getting active or more active. Make better choices like walking more or eating better.

OK, so you have been kind to yourself spiritually. Next, how can you be kind to your body?

_____
_____
_____
_____
_____
_____
_____
_____
_____
_____
_____
_____
_____
_____

Emotional Strength Workbook

Tracking Your Progress

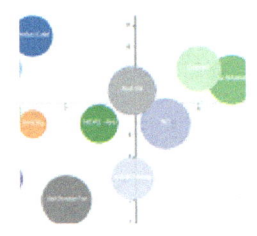

You could buy a journal dedicated just for your soul journey and write down where you are in each step of these categories, or you could take a picture of the next page and print it and start your journal this way.

Be sure to use your list of trusted people to keep those relationships intact. Research from Harvard University shows that people who have quality relationships with people and strong social support show greater happiness through life. It's through those experiences you will be able to test your **Emotional Strength**.

Step back and journal thoughts about your progress and how you think about the changes you have made. Are you stronger now? Can you do more to grow?

Emotional Strength Workbook

～

Be proud of all you have accomplished through the activities in this workbook, not matter how small. You can always begin again.

If you use it multiple times, or different versions, it will be good to compare through different ages and stages of your life. Reflection is good and helps you maintain your **Emotional Strength**. Each day, you can start anew.

～

Remember to be true to yourself and always **"You do you"**!

ABOUT THE AUTHOR

Alicia, who now only braves the dark northeastern winters, lives in New Jersey with her husband Mike and their children & fur babies. She juggles a safe office career and is CEO of successful businesses in Editing and Career Coaching while pursuing her lifelong passion of writing.

Alicia has lived through the dark of family dysfunction for twenty years before deciding to write books to inspire others. She hopes her books will help people battling the effects of confusion & complexity that stems from the chaos and dysfunction of the human condition, mental illness and abandonment. Her next book, her Memoir will help the undo false beliefs kids grow up with that cause shame, helplessness, hopelessness, and leave them feeling like there's something wrong with them. She knows it will help them be more open and live beyond the surface. Her writing is for anyone or anything citing fear, tension, and isolation due to the turbulent events of our time.

When she isn't writing, Alicia Pozsony enjoys taking pictures and walks, being a good parent and staying strong in her faith. Alicia also takes great pride in her civic duty by improving her community and helping shape and instill positivity in others and in the world as a Girl Scout leader, recently winning Outstanding Leader and Spirit awards.

Made in the USA
Coppell, TX
28 June 2022